ZOO ALBUM

To the memory of Dr John Kelly, Director of Taronga and Western Plains Zoos 1987–1997, and his guidance in the zoos' commitment to education and their excellence in conservation, care and presentation of wildlife — RM & AM

To Martin, Liam and Riley, with all my love — KL-D

ZOO ALBUM

Richard Morecroft and Alison Mackay
Illustrated by Karen Lloyd-Diviny

Enchanted Lion Books
New York

INTRODUCTION

Modern zoos are designed to be good for the animals that live in them, as well as enjoyable and interesting for humans to visit. They are places where animals can be studied and better understood. And the more we know about animals and their needs, the more we can look after them, both in zoos and in the wild.

Zoos are also places where creatures that are rare can be kept safe. If we can build up their numbers while they are in captivity, perhaps eventually they can be returned to the wild. For some types of animals this may mean the difference between survival and extinction.

Dedicated as they are to animals and nature, zoos are great places to learn about wildlife. Getting to know one animal individually makes it easier to care about lots of other animals like them. Zoos do a great job because they can introduce you to animals that you'd never otherwise meet.

But even when you walk around a zoo, there are still behind-the-scenes stories and bits of information you might not hear. This book shares some of those secrets with you, and helps you get to know the animals better. And since the keepers who look after the animals probably know them best of all, they tell their tales here as well.

This book is about real animals from real zoos. They're all at different ages and stages of life, and this is their "family album." It's a snapshot of a particular time. But there are animals like these in zoos all around the world; this book could just as easily be about the zoo near you. And, with any luck, it might encourage you to pay your local zoo a visit!

CONTENTS

Western Lowland Gorilla

Name: Haoko

Age: 4 years

Size: Slightly over 2 1/2 feet long (head and body length)

Weight: About 66 pounds

Size at birth: Nearly 12 inches long

Weight at birth: About 4 1/2 pounds

Food in the zoo: Mainly fruit and vegetables

Food in the wild: Fruit, plants, leaves and tree bark

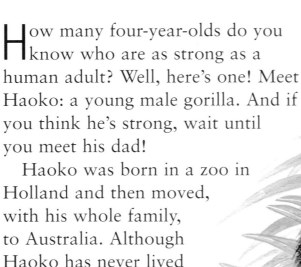

How many four-year-olds do you know who are as strong as a human adult? Well, here's one! Meet Haoko: a young male gorilla. And if you think he's strong, wait until you meet his dad!

Haoko was born in a zoo in Holland and then moved, with his whole family, to Australia. Although Haoko has never lived in the wild there are about 100,000 gorillas just like him that do. They're called Western Lowland Gorillas and they live in rainforests near the equator in the west of Africa. Their scientific name is one of the easiest to remember; it's *Gorilla gorilla gorilla*!

Haoko's family life is very much as it would be in the wild. They're a peaceful group which spends time looking for food and snoozing through the heat in the middle of the day. The youngsters play and explore, the females look after their

babies, and the dominant male keeps a watchful eye out for any problems.

At four years of age Haoko is old enough to start looking after himself. And that's just as well because his

Did You Know?

Haoko's family at the zoo have their own "hot rocks." These rocks are specially heated from below, so even when it's cold in winter the gorillas still have something warm to lie on.

mother, Mouila, has just had another baby and is busy caring for the new youngster. Haoko's playmates are two female gorillas called Kijivu and Shinda. For hours each day they climb and swing on ropes and branches, chase each other and play-fight. But although Haoko's mother may have other things on her mind, there's still someone keeping an eye on them — their father, Kibabu.

Kibabu is twenty years old and is the father of all the youngsters in the group. He's twice as big as the females and weighs around 485 pounds. That's more than the weight of two adult humans. Even more impressively, he has the strength of five or six men! It's easy to spot the adult males in a group and not just because of their size. When they become mature, at about twelve years old, the hair from their shoulders down to their thighs becomes silvery-white. Because of this, adult males are called silverbacks.

Kibabu is a good leader and despite his awesome strength he's not violent. His job is to look after the group. In the wild he would lead the group in looking for food, protect them from danger and find suitable places for them to build nests to rest in for the night. In the zoo his job is a bit easier — he doesn't have to search for food and there are no real threats, but he still has to keep his family group in order.

Did You Know?

Gorillas were first recognized as a species in 1847 by a naturalist called Dr. Savage. He was given a large skull by a missionary and, realizing it was different from a chimpanzee's, gave it a new scientific name.

And with Haoko's boisterous nature Kibabu sometimes has to lay down the law quite firmly. If he must, he will bite or hit one of the group when they misbehave, but most of the time he only has to grunt in a threatening way or even just "give them the look." The whole family treats him with great respect.

Relatively Speaking

It's not hard to see how similar gorillas are to humans. They have hands (rather than paws) with which they eat their food and groom each other; the youngsters play together and annoy the adults with their rough-and-tumble games. They even make faces, like us, to show how they're feeling, and in many other ways their behavior reminds us of our own.

Humans and gorillas are both members of the animal family called the "Great Apes" along with chimpanzees and orang-utans. Nearly 98% of what makes up gorillas also makes up humans, so gorillas are more like us than not like us! Researchers in America have even taught a female gorilla, named Koko, to talk to them using sign language. Koko knows over 1,000 different signs.

Gorillas are vegetarians

The Keeper Says …

"Haoko is at a mischievous age and seems to think that keepers are fair game. If there's a keeper nearby when he's going to the toilet he will try to aim at us — he's even tried to pee in our rubber boots! Haoko likes making a lot of noise — hitting the wire, beating his chest and banging on the walls. One of the things he loves most are "gorilla balls." We make them up out of oats, Weetbix and honey, and they're delicious enough to keep even Haoko quiet for a few minutes."

Libby Kartzoff, GORILLA KEEPER

Sumatran Tiger

Name: Selatan

Age: 8 years (adult female)

Size: About 8 feet long

Weight: 200 pounds (about the weight of a large man)

Size at birth: About 9 3/4 inches long

Weight at birth: Less than 2 1/4 pounds

Food in the zoo: Meat! Chicken, kangaroo or beef

Food in the wild: Pig or deer

Now she's had cubs of her own and, as a full-grown female tiger, weighs about 200 pounds. Her mate's name is Shiva and, although he's bigger and heavier than Selatan, he's nowhere near as brave. The keepers say he's quite easily frightened!

When Selatan had her first cub she didn't produce enough milk, so it

When Selatan was born, she was the size of a guinea pig. Her eyes were closed and she weighed only around 2 pounds.

Did You Know?

Tigers "prustinate." It's one of the ways in which tigers communicate and it's a sort of blowy-growly purr while they rub cheeks together.

needed to be looked after by the keepers. They fed it from a bottle and the baby soon became strong and healthy. Since then Selatan has had three male cubs and has managed to feed them all. The biggest one is nicknamed "Pepper" after his keeper. Pepper was a bit cheeky when he was young and would run out of the nursery pen if the

The Keeper Says …

"Selatan isn't afraid of the keepers and can sometimes be aggressive. But she also shows affection and enjoys having her head scratched. Even though she's an adult she can still be playful — sometimes she torments Shiva by pouncing on him or hitting him with her paws!

"I talk a lot to the tigers and I think they know me quite well. When I returned after being away on vacation for a few weeks the tigers prustinated as soon as they heard my voice and then came straight over to see me."

David Pepper-Edwards ("Pepper"),
Tiger Keeper

keeper was nearby … and then playfully bite him!

There were once eight different types of tiger in various parts of the world. Now there are only five because some have become extinct. (Tigers have often been killed by humans for their skins, for meat, for sport, and for use in some traditional medicines.) Sumatran Tigers are the smallest of the five types, and their home in the wild is the tropical island of Sumatra, in Indonesia. During the day it can be very hot, so the tigers often rest lying down in shallow rivers to stay cool. This might seem strange because cats don't usually like to get wet!

Fighting Extinction

With only about 300–400 Sumatran Tigers still living in the wild, zoos have an important job to do. There are now about 180 Sumatran Tigers in zoos around the world, many of which — like Selatan's cubs — were actually born in captivity. Selatan and her cubs are part of an international effort to make sure the Sumatran Tiger doesn't become extinct.

As Wide as Your Whiskers

Tigers' whiskers don't only look spectacular, they're important to help tigers feel their way around. The whiskers are the same width as the tiger's body, so the tiger knows that if its whiskers fit through a space its body will too.

High-tech Tigers

Selatan's three cubs carry special "name-tags." Each cub has its own microchip implanted just below the skin. These microchips can be "read," like barcodes in a supermarket, and give information about each cub. The keepers don't need the micro-chips to tell who's who, however. They know the cubs so well they just have to check the dots and stripes on their tails!

Tigers are carnivores

13

Black Rhino

Name: Kusomona

Age: 15 months

Size: About 8 - 11 1/2 feet long (as an adult)

Weight: 3,100 pounds (as an adult)

Size at birth: About the size of a labrador dog

Weight at birth: 66 - 88 pounds

Food in the zoo: Branches and leaves, also hay, apples, carrots and bread

Food in the wild: Branches and leaves

Rhinos are the world's second largest land animal (elephants are the largest). Adult males can weigh as much as a family-size car!

Rhinos need to eat a lot — about 66 pounds of food each day — to keep their huge bodies going.

Kusomona's parents lived in the wild in Zimbabwe, Southern Africa, before they were brought to the zoo. Kusomona means "first born" in the tribal language where they were captured and he was given this name because he was the first rhino born into captivity in Australia for nearly 22 years.

Kusomona will stay close to his mother until he is around 2 1/2 years old, and she will show him what to eat, how to sharpen his horn, roll in the mud and protect himself. After this time he will have to fend for himself as she may well have another calf on the way.

In the wild they browse on leaves, buds, small trees or bushes. In the zoo they also are given apples, carrots, sweet potatoes, some horse feed and, as a treat, whole loaves of bread.

Although they have a sharp sense of smell and good hearing, rhinos have very poor eyesight. If you were standing very still, a rhino probably wouldn't see you until it was less than 33 yards away — although it would smell or hear you long before that.

On the Horns of a Dilemma

Rhinos have one or two incredibly tough horns that grow between their forehead and their nose. These horns aren't bone (like cows' horns), but are made of keratin — the same stuff that makes up hair, fingernails and claws. Male rhinos use their horns to defend their territory and to fight with other males over mates. Both males and females use their horns for gathering food: they uproot shrubs, knock down branches and push over trees with them.

Unfortunately, the horn is also the biggest threat to the rhino's survival.

Did You Know?

Rhinos use mud as an insect repellent. They roll around in muddy water and as the mud dries on their skins it not only helps keep them cool but protects them against biting flies.

were about 65,000 Black Rhinos in South Africa; today there are less than 2,000, and this number is still dropping. Soon there may be no Black Rhinos alive in the wild at all, which is why it's so important that zoos look after them in captivity.

Black and White

There are two kinds of rhinos in Africa — the Black Rhino and the White Rhino — but they're both actually gray in color. They're both about the same size, and they both have two horns. So how do you tell them apart? Well, it's all to do with the shape of their faces. The Black Rhino has a long, pointed upper lip which it uses to grab leaves and branches from bushes and low trees. The White Rhino

Rhino horn is used as a medicine in some countries and to make ornaments in others. It's worth a lot of money and so poachers are willing to take great risks in hunting and killing rhinos for their horns. Twenty years ago there

has a wide, square-shaped mouth for grazing on grasses and other plants on the ground.

Scent Marking

In the wild, rhinos stamp in their own droppings and then walk around their territory. With every step they take they leave behind their own special smell which lets other rhinos know to whom the print belongs.

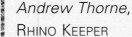
Zoo food for rhinos

The Keeper Says …

"We nicknamed Kusomona "Little Man" when he was born because he looked like an old man, tottering about with his big, loose coat hanging off him. Now he's a huge bouncing ball of energy! He enjoys running into his mother and headbutting her when she's asleep. He also annoys her by climbing onto her and trying to steal her food. He's quite confident and often a bit cheeky — he even makes mock charges at us keepers.

"He likes being scratched behind the ears and under the chin and neck. His favorite food is bananas — whole bananas, with their skins still on! On warm days Kusomona and his mother laze in the sun. When it's really hot they keep cool by rolling in the nearest patch of mud."

Andrew Thorne,
RHINO KEEPER

Tasmanian Devil

Name: Yanga

Age: 5 years (adult female)

Size: About 23 1/2 inches long (the size of a small dog)

Weight: 15 1/2 pounds

Size at birth: Between 1/4 and 1/3 inch long (smaller than a jelly bean)

Weight at birth: .008 ounces

Food in the zoo: Rats, chicks, eggs and bones

Food in the wild: Carrion (dead birds and mammals), and sometimes live birds or possums

Tasmanian Devils are probably best known around the world as cartoon creatures with huge teeth and a talent for becoming a noisy tornado. Well, Yanga, like all Tasmanian Devils, does have a big mouth with strong teeth and she can make some loud noises, but she never turns into a whirlwind! In fact, she spends most of her day snoozing and then wanders around at night looking for food. And since devils mainly eat dead animals, they are not really fierce hunters.

Occasionally they might grab a bird sleeping in its nest, but mostly they like the sort of dinner that doesn't put up a fight.

That doesn't mean that Yanga is always calm and quiet, however. Sometimes the keepers want to introduce her to a male devil, but they know Yanga is very protective of her territory. When a male arrives in her home patch, she hisses, screams and growls, opening her mouth wide to show all her teeth. Then she hits him around the face with her paws and quite often makes his nose bleed! This seems to be a normal part of getting to know each other, devil-style, because she's had three babies with one male whom she attacked like this.

Although Yanga's natural home is the often-cool Australian island of Tasmania, she loves to get really warm. So the keepers have put a heat lamp in her enclosure and she spends many happy hours basking beneath it.

The Keeper Says …

"Yanga lives very much as she would in the wild. We don't need to handle her so we try to leave her undisturbed. She's a very good scavenger and we encourage her natural skills by dragging her food around her enclosure then hiding it in a different place each night. She follows the trail and always finds it!"

Gary Fry, AUSTRALIAN MAMMALS KEEPER

Yanga eats chicks

Did You Know?

Aboriginal rock art in Kakadu (in the Northern Territory) from 500 years ago shows Tasmanian Devils. This suggests they once lived all over Australia, but may have been wiped out on the mainland by dingoes, Australia's only native dog, both wild and carnivorous.

Yanga the Gardener

Once, one of the keepers spent hours dressing up Yanga's enclosure with new plants, branches and leaves. That night, Yanga pulled down all the branches, dug up all the plants, made a big nest from the leaves that she liked and pushed the rest of the wreckage into her pond! She was not popular the next day.

Parents with Pouches

When people think of marsupials (mammals with pouches) it's most often kangaroos or koalas that come to

mind. But Tasmanian Devils are marsupials too. At birth, marsupial babies are tiny; newborn Tasmanian Devils are only about the size of a large bee. They crawl through their mother's fur into her pouch and stay there feeding on milk until they grow big enough to start exploring the outside world.

Short-beaked Echidna

Name: Spike

Age: Over 6 years (adult female)

Size: About 1 1/3 feet long

Weight: About 10 pounds

Size at hatching: 1/2 inch (about the size of a jelly bean)

Weight at hatching: .013 ounces

Food in the zoo: Ants and other insects, worms (meal, earth or red), also minced meat, raw eggs and olive oil

Food in the wild: Ants, termites and other insects

It's hard to imagine a more fitting name for an echidna than Spike. Spike is covered in them (spikes, that is) and they're very good protection against anything that might want to eat her. If she's frightened or threatened she simply tucks her long nose in and rolls up into a ball. All her spines stick out and her head and soft belly are protected. Sometimes, if an echidna is on loose ground when it's threatened,

it uses its strong legs and claws to push out the soil underneath it. Very quickly, its legs and head disappear, leaving only its spiky back above the surface. If a curious dingo (Australia's native wild dog) or big goanna (monitor lizard) are sniffing around hungrily, they'll probably get their noses spiked!

However, echidnas don't spend all their time being scared. An echidna's day is mainly taken up with searching for food like ants, termites, grubs or worms. The echidna pokes and prods with its long nose, exploring cracks in the ground and holes in rotten logs. It has a very good sense of smell and once it has caught the scent of, say, a termite nest, it will burrow and dig with its claws until it finds the termites. Then a long, thin (and very sticky) tongue whips in and out of its mouth, picking up the little insects.

Sometimes Spike meets groups of children at the zoo's Education Center. The children sit quietly in a circle on the ground with Spike in the middle. She wanders around, sniffing shoes and hands and sometimes licking fingers, leaving a trail of sticky echidna saliva behind!

Aussie Egg-layers

The echidna is a very special type of egg-laying mammal called a monotreme. The only other egg-laying mammal in the world (the platypus) also lives in Australia. The eggs of the echidna and the platypus are soft and leathery — more like reptile eggs than the hard-shelled eggs of birds.

The female echidna lays a single egg after burrowing into a protected place like a hollow under a log or rock. When the baby hatches it looks like a wrinkly bag of

Did You Know?

Echidnas don't have teeth but their tongues are 4 - 6 inches long. That's about as long as your hand, but much more sticky!

pink skin. The mother feeds it with her milk and it stays in a pouch on her body for about three months, growing bigger and eventually getting small spines. Then it's time to leave the pouch before its mother gets a bad case of prickled tummy!

Lining Up for Love

When a female echidna is ready to get together with a male, she gives off a special scent. This usually happens around July or August and may attract up to seven or eight males from some distance away. The female just keeps strolling along and the males follow,

The Keeper Says …

"Spike is an inquisitive animal. She's not too timid and doesn't usually mind being held — although once when I was holding her so a photographer could take some pictures, she got a bit nervous and tried to bury herself in my arms by digging. It wasn't very comfortable!"

Gary Fry, AUSTRALIAN MAMMALS KEEPER

Spike's dinner bowl

forming a line behind her. This goes on for hours or even up to a couple of days. One by one the males give up their place in the line and leave. Eventually there's only one male echidna left, and the female knows he's the one for her!

Did You Know?

The female echidna has to bury herself upside down in the ground for mating. Otherwise her spines would injure the male while they mate.

Little Penguin

Name: CB (or Cee Bee)

Age: 7–8 months

Size: 1 1/3 - 1 1/2 feet long

Weight: 2 1/4 pounds

Size at birth: About 2 3/4 inches long

Weight at birth: A penguin egg weighs about 2 ounces

Food in the zoo and in the wild: Fishy things, like pilchards, squid, sardines and anchovies

Little Penguins are the smallest of all penguins. They live around the southern half of Australia and around the North and South Islands of New Zealand. You may sometimes hear them called Fairy Penguins, and although this is a popular name, Little Penguin is actually the correct one.

CB is one of 30 Little Penguins that live at the zoo. The keepers call CB

"her," but in fact they don't know for sure if she's a she or a he! It's very hard for the keepers to find out a penguin's gender until it's at least four years old and even then it can be difficult because it doesn't show any outside signs of being male or female. However, the keepers are able to recognize each of the penguins from their behavior and appearance, and they all have their own names.

CB was hatched at the zoo and was looked after by the keepers while she

Did You Know?

Penguins can sleep lying down or standing up. They take short naps of three to four minutes in their burrows or in sheltered spots.

was very young. Being a parent is hard work for a Little Penguin so although the female lays two eggs at a time, usually only one chick will survive to become an adult. CB's chances of survival were much better if the keepers looked after her themselves.

Haven't You Grown!

In the wild, chicks are looked after inside a burrow dug by the adult penguins in loose ground or in sand dunes close to the sea's edge. The adult penguins spend their days at sea, hunting for small fish. In the evening they regurgitate food and then feed it to their chicks from beak to beak. The chicks will be fed like this for about eight weeks and as they grow they need more and more food. By the end of this time the parents can only just manage to come up with enough food for themselves and the chicks. When the chicks leave the nest they're normally quite a bit heavier than their parents — after all, they've just been sitting in the burrow eating while their parents have been out all day fishing!

The Keeper Says …

"CB is always easy to find as she loves following the keepers around and she's usually the first one at the gate for feeding and talk time. She seems to look on the keepers as her best friends and loves being petted and held — sometimes she even tries to follow us out of the enclosure! She's great for helping us to teach people about Little Penguins.

"CB was hand-raised by one of our keepers called Clare Henderson. Her nickname is "Care Bear" so we used those initials and that's how CB got her name. Because she spent so much time with her keeper when she was very young, CB is still getting used to the company of penguins rather than humans. She still hangs out with the other hand-raised youngsters and it's taking a while for her to become part of the penguin group. This is a challenge with any hand-raised animal and it usually just takes time and patience to introduce them back to their natural companions."

Elle Bombanado, AQUATIC MAMMALS KEEPER

Did You Know?

Penguins actually "fly" under the water. Their flippers are just like wings and propel them forward while they use their feet as rudders to change direction.

Penguins eat mainly fish

Swimming Feathers

Penguins' feathers are very important in the water. Adults have two different types of feathers: short, stiff ones lying close together on the surface and overlapping (a bit like scales) and soft, downy ones next to their skin to keep them warm. The penguins keep the top set well waterproofed with oil from a special gland near their tail. But young penguins aren't waterproof. It takes them twenty days to shed their fluffy feathers and grow a new, sleek, sea-going set.

29

Andean Condor

Name: Bruce

Age: 18 years (could live to 50 years)

Size: 3 3/4 feet tall, nearly 10 foot wingspan

Weight: Up to nearly 26 1/2 pounds

Size at birth: About the size of a pigeon

Weight at birth: Just about 1/2 pound

Food in the zoo and in the wild: Dead mice, rabbits, baby rats (he especially likes eyeballs!)

It wasn't long ago that Bruce the Andean Condor was afraid of heights. It may seem strange that a huge bird, which in the wild soars to almost 3 3/4 miles above the ground, would be nervous about gliding only .03 miles or so up in the air. But Bruce had spent most of his eighteen years in a cage,

with little chance to test his flying skills. Now he takes part, with other birds, in a display of free flying watched by visitors to the zoo.

Bruce has an enormous 10 foot wingspan and is certainly the biggest bird in the display. In the wild, Andean Condors use their huge wings to glide

Did You Know?

You can see through a condor's nostrils. If you look at a condor side-on you'll see a clear nostril hole at the top of its beak that you can look straight through.

The Keeper Says …

"Bruce is very curious and always interested in exploring new objects, like poking around in a bucket. Somehow his face seems really expressive, which may sound rather unusual for a bird. When I was first teaching him to fly I'm sure I saw a look of terror just before he took off! It was as if he was saying, 'You want me to do WHAT?'

"He's a quick learner, though. Now he soars on the updrafts of air with much more confidence and he'll land on a tree stump if I point at it. He'll even walk into a crate if he needs to be transported somewhere … and he didn't like doing that to start with!

"If it's a fine day, Bruce loves to sit on a branch and spread out his huge wings to soak up the warmth of the sun."

Dinah Monroe, BIRD KEEPER

and soar for hours, scanning the mountain slopes and valleys for food. They eat mainly dead animals and seem to enjoy the innards most of all. Unlike hawks and eagles, they hardly ever hunt living creatures.

Bruce lives in a large cage with his sister Connie. Sometimes you can hear them "talking" to each other using low hisses and croaks. Even though they're brother and sister they have very different personalities. Connie is often rather grumpy and has sometimes bitten her keepers when they've been feeding her. But Bruce is very well behaved and never aggressive.

Bruce eats rabbits

Did You Know?

Andean Condors are the largest flying birds of prey in the world. Because they're so big it's very difficult for them to launch off the ground without running. Sometimes they use a breeze to help them lift off.

A Curious Habit

Like many birds, condors have white, runny droppings. To help keep themselves cool on a hot day, they actually let these wet droppings splash over their legs and feet. So if you see Bruce with rather messy legs, it wasn't an accident — he probably meant to do it.

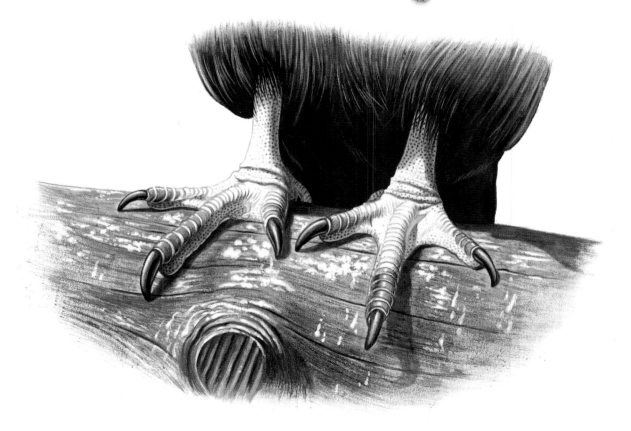

Komodo Dragon

Name: Ora

Age: 45 years (could live to 60 or 70 years)

Size: About 10 feet (adult male)

Weight: About 220 pounds (adult male)

Size at hatching: About 15 1/2 inches

Weight at hatching: 1/5 of a pound

Food in the zoo: Mainly chickens

Food in the wild: Rodents, other reptiles and anything they can catch

Ora hatched from an egg on the Indonesian island of Komodo 45 years ago. The dragons are kings and queens of the island and "Ora" is the word for Komodo Dragon in the local language. Humans have to be very careful around these giant reptiles. They are afraid of

This is Ora, the Komodo Dragon. Komodo Dragons are the biggest lizards in the world, with some of them growing up to nearly 13 feet in length.

nothing, and humans (especially children) could make a tasty meal!

In the zoo, though, Ora has become quite friendly with his keeper and particularly likes having his eyelids gently scratched. That really relaxes him. He also loves basking on one of his specially heated rocks or under the heat lamp in his undercover den. Ora hates cold winter rain

Did You Know?

Komodo Dragons can swim. Although they tend to stay mainly on Komodo, some dragons have been seen on nearby islands … and they certainly didn't get there by boat!

so when it's chilly and wet, you can be sure he will be snug in his cave, stretched out under the heater.

Ora's favorite food is chicken, but he likes them whole: feathers, bones and all. In fact, whether it's chicken or rats, the fur, feathers and bones are necessary for Ora to digest his food properly.

When Ora is wandering around, his long, forked tongue flicks in and out of his mouth every few seconds. Just like snakes, Komodo Dragons can "smell" with their tongues. They rely on smell much more than eyesight to track down their dinner. Although they certainly hunt living prey (like wild pigs), more often Komodo Dragons eat carrion: the rotting flesh of animals that have died. It has been said that Komodo Dragons have the worst-smelling breath in the world! It also means that a bite from a Komodo Dragon can be very dangerous because of all the germs in its mouth.

Ora eats the feathers, bones and all

Did You Know?

The local Indonesians sometimes tell stories of people mysteriously disappearing on Komodo. Who knows if it has anything to do with the dragons … would you want to find out?

A Walk on the Wild Side

A couple of years ago, Ora had to be moved from his old cage on the other side of the zoo to the new enclosure he now lives in. Instead of packing him up in a box, the keeper decided Ora could walk along the paths through the zoo.

Every few feet, the keeper put bits of meat on the pathway so Ora would head in the right direction. Lots of people came to watch the Komodo Dragon out for a stroll, but even with so many tasty human legs around, he was very well behaved.

The Keeper Says …

"I've worked with all sorts of reptiles and I'm pretty sure that Komodo Dragons are the most intelligent. They seem to learn quickly about a new environment and Ora certainly seems to recognize me and one or two of the other keepers. If we take a stranger into the enclosure, Ora will ignore us keepers and go straight towards the stranger, flicking his tongue in and out to sample the new smell.

"Ora's complete lack of fear means he's quite calm. Even if we have to give him injections or take blood samples to check his health, he doesn't flinch. We have half a dozen keepers ready to hold him still but they're not usually needed. Perhaps he thinks he needs to show us how tough he is!"

Terry Boylan, REPTILE KEEPER

Green Anaconda

- **Name:** Ana
- **Age:** 30-something years
- **Size:** 13 feet long
- **Weight:** 81 1/2 pounds
- **Size at birth:** 31 1/2 inches
- **Weight at birth:** 2/3 of a pound
- **Food in the zoo and in the wild:** Rats, rats and more rats!

Ana is a big snake — a *very* big snake. She's about 13 feet long, and Green Anacondas like her can grow up to 16 1/2 or even 19 1/2 feet. Although some other types of snakes may grow a bit longer, anacondas usually have thick, heavy bodies. When it comes to sheer bulk, anacondas are reckoned to be the biggest snakes in the world. Mind you, it would depend on whether you weighed one with a recent meal inside its stomach, because these snakes can swallow a pig or a deer in a single gulp!

Did You Know?

Anacondas can climb trees. In the wild, they will sometimes hang in the low branches of trees and then drop on their prey as it passes underneath!

When Ana was born in a zoo overseas, she was already about 3 feet long. Anacondas don't lay eggs like most snakes but have live babies. Lots of them! So Ana could have had as many as 60 brothers and sisters all the same age. Ana is over 30 years old now and, although she may live to around 40, she's definitely an elderly snake. Also, as the only anaconda in Australia, she's already quite famous.

In the zoo she doesn't eat very often; over one or two weeks, she'll eat three rats. In the wild, anacondas sometimes eat much larger creatures, like deer. Then they don't eat again for weeks while they digest the big lump inside their stomachs.

The rats Ana eats are already dead, but if she had to kill her prey in the wild she'd coil her body around it and squeeze. This doesn't crush the prey, it just stops its breathing so it dies of suffocation. Constrictor snakes, like Ana, have quite big teeth for grabbing their prey, but they don't have any poison.

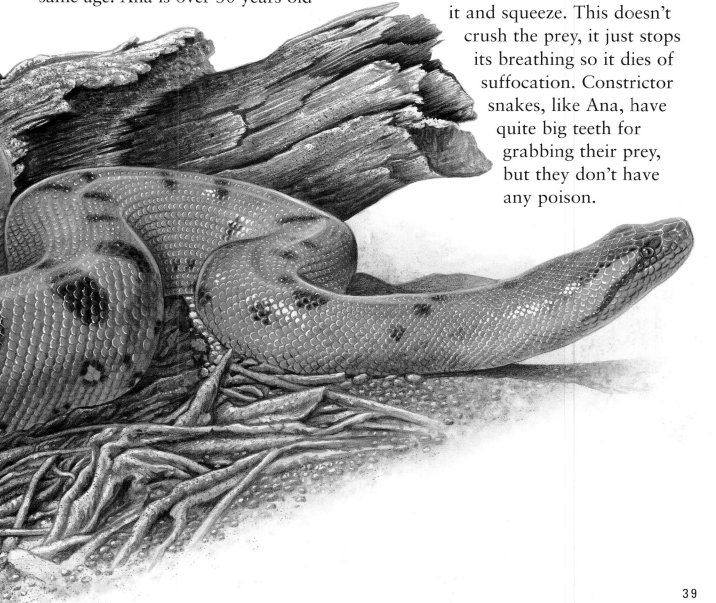

Open Wide …

Even though an anaconda is a huge snake, its head is only about the size of your foot. So how could it swallow

something as big as a pig or a deer? Well, like all snakes, Ana's lower jawbones come apart easily. Once she's got a grip on something with her backward-pointing teeth, she can stretch open her mouth and throat to form a wide tube that even an enormous dinner can slide into. As the food passes down toward her stomach, her jawbones go back into their normal position and her throat returns to its usual slim shape.

Rats, rats, rats!

The Keeper Says …

"Ana doesn't seem too worried about us moving around in her enclosure. She doesn't hiss or try to bite us, but she's often quite curious. Sometimes she creeps up silently behind us to see what we're doing and then we get a surprise because we didn't know she was there! If she gets too close we push her away gently with a broom.

"Like most snakes, Ana's rather ticklish. If she's sliding over an unfamiliar surface, you can see the scales on her tummy shudder a little."

Michael Muscat, REPTILE KEEPER

Snake Pool

In the wild, an anaconda spends most of its time in water. The large spots on its body make it very difficult to see as it lies submerged with only its eyes and nose above the surface. It grabs unwary animals looking for a drink and drags them into the water.

Ana spends much of her time in water too. Her pool in the zoo has a glass side so that visitors can see her hiding under the water. The pool has to be kept warm — the same sort of temperature as a tropical South

Did You Know?

While a new home was being built for her at the zoo, Ana lived in a room kept warm with heaters and lazed around in a large bathtub full of water!

American river — so that Ana's metabolism works properly and she stays healthy.

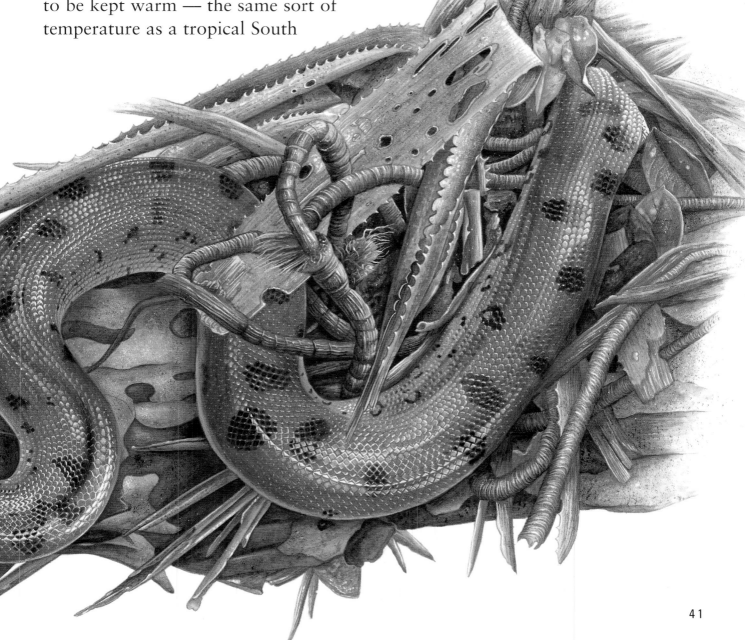

Poison Arrow Frog

Name: Golden Crown

Age: 3 years (adult male)

Size: 1 - 1 1/2 inches

Weight: .35 ounces (females are a bit bigger)

Size as tadpole: Tiny! 1/2 - 1 inch

Weight as tadpole: 0.003 ounces (hardly there at all!)

Food in the zoo and in the wild: Insects, including maggots, flies and crickets

Deep in the Amazon rainforest the local South American people make frog kebabs. But they're not for eating. As the brightly colored frogs get cooked they release poison from glands in their skin. The locals use this poison on the tips of their arrows and darts for hunting — it's so strong that it can

paralyze small animals, like birds and monkeys almost instantly. This is why they are called Poison Arrow Frogs.

In the zoo these little frogs don't have to worry about ending up on the end of a skewer. They live in an enclosure that is like a miniature tropical rainforest. It's kept warm and wet and there are sheltering plants, like bromeliads, for protection. Bromeliads have spiky leaves and collect water in their bowl-like centers. They act like swimming pools for the tadpoles. It takes about ten to twelve weeks for the tadpoles to become fully developed frogs and leave the bromeliad pool behind.

Poison Arrow Frogs don't really have families — the males and females only get together to mate and then go their separate ways. Even in the zoo, though, males such as Golden Crown like to establish their own territory. They decide who's in charge by nudging and wrestling each other. The loser submits by bowing his head, while the winner lifts up his body with his head and legs stretched out.

Did You Know?

Some male Poison Arrow Frogs will stand guard over fertilized eggs, peeing on them to keep them wet. When the tadpoles hatch, the frog puts them on its back and carries them to the nearest bromeliad plant where they can develop in its pool of water.

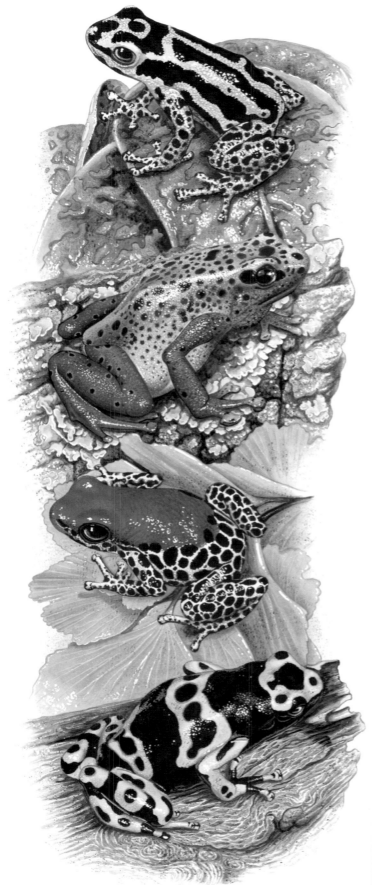

Truth or Dare?

Most frogs are green, brown or gray so that they blend into their surroundings, but Poison Arrow Frogs are vividly colored. Most are jet black with canary yellow, bright red or cobalt blue markings, so although they're still hard to see because they're so small, their colors really stand out. You might think that a frog which makes such a show of itself is asking to be eaten — in fact, it's not. Its bright colors warn predators that it is poisonous and not

The Keeper Says …

"The Poison Arrow Frogs dislike strong sunlight. They need somewhere shady and wet to hide so that their skin doesn't dry out. Their natural habitat in the Amazon rainforest is very damp and humid, so to make the zoo space feel like home they need to have their own "rain." It's my job to provide the rain by spraying the frogs' home with water once a day.

"I also have to make sure the frogs have enough of the right kind of food. Poison Arrow Frogs are carnivores — they eat only live meat, mainly insects. In the zoo they eat flightless fruit flies, maggots and hatchling crickets. They spend most of their day hunting for these delicacies."

Dion Hobcroft, REPTILE KEEPER

a good meal. But funnily enough this isn't always true. In fact, only three out of the 40 different kinds of Poison Arrow Frog are extremely poisonous. So the other 37 species are bluffing, borrowing the danger signs of their genuinely poisonous relatives.

Did You Know?

Poison Arrow Frogs (as well as other varieties of frogs) don't only repel creatures that may want to eat them. Their bodies also make chemicals to defend them against types of fungus and bacteria that would love to grow on their moist skin.

Frogs eat small insects

GLOSSARY

AMPHIBIAN An animal whose body temperature depends on the temperature of its surroundings. Amphibians usually have soft, slimy skin and spend the first part of their life in water.

AQUATIC Lives mainly in water.

BIRD A warm-blooded animal which lays eggs and has wings and feathers.

BROMELIADS Spiky-leaved plants that collect water in a "bowl" in their centers.

BROWSE Plant-eating animals browse on the leaves and branches of trees or shrubs, but graze on types of grass.

CARNIVORE A meat eater (herbivores eat plants).

CARRION Dead meat! Food from the bodies of dead animals.

CONSTRICTOR A type of snake that kills its prey by coiling tightly around it and squeezing.

ENVIRONMENT All the ingredients of a place: the land, the weather, the plants and the animals.

EXTINCTION When all the members of a particular species have died out.

FUNGUS and BACTERIA Lifeforms that can grow on or in parts of an animal's body and make it ill.

GREAT APES A group of mammals comprising gorillas, orang-utans, chimpanzees and humans.

HABITAT The particular environment in which an animal lives.

KERATIN The substance of which hair, claws, fingernails and rhino horns are made.

MAMMAL A warm-blooded animal that produces milk for its young. Mammals are usually furry.

MARSUPIAL A mammal with a pouch for its young to develop in, such as kangaroos, wombats and Tasmanian Devils.

METABOLISM The way a creature's body gets energy from its food.

MICROCHIP A tiny device holding information, usually made of silicon and metal, which can be put under an animal's skin to help identify it.

MONOTREME An egg-laying mammal. The only monotremes are the echidna and the platypus.

PREDATOR A creature that hunts another creature for food.

RAINFOREST A forest that depends on heavy rainfall. Most rainforests have very shallow soil.

REGURGITATE To bring food back up that has been swallowed. Birds do this to feed their young.

REPTILE An animal who has scales and whose body temperature depends on the temperature of its surroundings.

SILVERBACK An adult male gorilla whose back and thighs are covered with silvery hair.

WINGSPAN The distance from one wingtip to another when the wings are stretched out.

Acknowledgements

This book would not have been possible without the support and cooperation of the staff of Taronga Zoo, Western Plains Zoo and Melbourne Zoo. We thank sincerely: Darril Clements, Scott Sloan, Anita Nelving and Mark Williams of Taronga Zoo Public Relations; Tracey Crawford of Western Plains Zoo Public Relations; Ailsa McOscar (Communications Assistant) and Colin Van Dyk (Food Store Manager) of Melbourne Zoo.

Thank you to all ...

The animals	and their keepers:
Haoko, the Western Lowland Gorilla	Libby Kartzoff
Selatan, the Sumatran Tiger	David Pepper-Edwards
Kusomona, the Black Rhino	Andrew Thorne
Yanga, the Tasmanian Devil	
Spike, the Short-beaked Echidna	Gary Fry
CB, the Little Penguin	Elle Bombanado
Bruce, the Andean Condor	Dinah Monroe
Ora, the Komodo Dragon	Terry Boylan and Jason Langdale
Ana, the Green Anaconda	Michael Muscat
Golden Crown, the Poison Arrow Frog	Dion Hobcroft

... and special thanks to Jeanne Walker for her research skills.

Finally, thanks to Margaret Wild and David Francis for starting this book on its journey, to Ali Lavau and Lisa Riley for guiding it along the way, and Gabrielle Bonney for patiently bringing it to publication.

First American Edition published in 2004 by
Enchanted Lion Books, 201 Richards Street, Brooklyn, NY 11231

Second Hardcover Printing, 2008
First Paperback Printing, 2008

Library of Congress Cataloging-in-Publication Data
Morecroft, Richard.
Zoo album / by Richard Morecroft and Alison Mackay; illustrated by Karen
Lloyd-Diviny. — 1st American ed.
 p. cm.
ISBN: 1-59270-032-2 (ISBN 13: 978-1-59270-032-5)
1. Zoo animals—Juvenile literature. I. Mackay, Alison. II. Lloyd-Diviny,
Karen, ill. III. Title.
QL77.5.M67 2004
590.73—dc22   2004043262

ISBN 13: 978-1-59270-104-9 / ISBN 10: 1-59270-104-3 paperback

Designed and typeset by Kerry Klinner
The illustrations were painted and drawn with watercolor,
    gouache and colored pencils
Color reproduction by Colorwize, Adelaide
Printed in Hong Kong by Quality Printing

Resources

http://WWW.AZA.ORG: The American Zoo & Aquarium Association's online database of accredited zoos and aquariums, with links to the websites of zoos and aquariums around the U.S.A., as well as information about volunteering, adopting an animal, and supporting wildlife conservation world wide. Also includes a photo gallery, and web links for kids.

http://NATZOO.SI.EDU: The Smithsonian National Zoological Park's website, with loads of information about animals, conservation and science, educational programs and projects, and more.

http://NETVET.WUSTL.EDU/E-ZOO.HTM: The website for the electronic zoo, with information about animals, organizations, related publications, and more. Further, a list of links to conservation, environmental and wildlife organizations can be obtained by going to http:/NETVET.WUSTL.EDU/CONSERVE.HTM.

http://WWW.NWF.ORG: The National Wildlife Federation's site provides information about its programs as well as about wildlife and how to take action on the environment. The site also has a "KidZone," full of information, pictures and projects.

http://WCS.ORG: The Wildlife Conservation Society's website, with information about the animals, programs and events at New York City zoos as well as at the New York Aquarium. This site also provides information about animals in the wild, endangered animals and more.